The Little Book of
CANDLE POWER

*Lessons in Lighting Your Life with Candles
and Their Colors*

CARLI LOGAN

Photographs by Paul Rocheleau

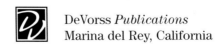

DeVorss *Publications*
Marina del Rey, California

DeVorss Publications
Marina del Rey, California

The Little Book of Candle Power
© 2002 Carli Logan

ISBN: 0-87516-780-2
Library of Congress Control Number: 2002102824

DeVorss & Company, *Publishers*
Box 550
Marina del Rey CA 90294-0550
www.devorss.com

Printed in China

THIS IS A BOOK ABOUT CANDLES

and the beauty they lend to the power of affirmative thought—healing, helping and altering your life permanently for the better.

In his book *Candles in the Roman Rite*, scholar-cleric Edwin Ryan observes:

The ceremonial use of light is ancient and widespread. In at least two religions, the Brahman and the Parsi, light is itself an object of worship. In other non-Christian cults it figures prominently as part of the ceremonial . . . the Mohammedans use lighted lamps to mark places or objects of especial sanctity, and in the Kaa'ba in Mecca a myriad of lamps are lighted. The ancient Greeks, the Romans and the Incas of Peru had their Sacred Fire, and the Greek torch race originated in ceremonies connected with the relighting of this Fire. . . . In Egypt lights were kept ever burning before the statues of Isis. . . .

In the Jewish ritual also lights were employed. Before the Holy of Holies stood a seven-branched candlestick containing lamps always burning; in the Outer Court also stood an altar whereon the Holy Fire was never suffered to go out; illumination formed part of the ritual in the feast of the Tabernacles. . . .

The Romans and other Latin-speaking Christians came ultimately to adopt symbolic lighting. . . . To attach symbolic meaning to ceremonial and to objects connected therewith is in itself sound and justifiable and within reasonable limits is to be encouraged.

4

Our present-day "symbolic lights" are, and for centuries have been, Candles. These relatively small, easily manageable and safe items are also the modern-day equivalent of the ancient "Fires." When these Fires and Candles were lighted, there were not only flames but also *words*—words intended to *change the course of things,* to bring help and healing. We do the same today.

"For thou wilt light my candle: the Lord my
God will enlighten my darkness."

Psalm 18:28

"If thy whole body therefore be full of light,
having no part dark, the whole shall be full of
light, as when the bright shining of a candle
doth give thee light."

Luke 11:36

Lighting Your Thought

THE RITUAL OF CANDLE-LIGHTING

is a powerful medium that you can use in the creative process of *lighting your thinking*—which means *lighting your life*. This ancient practice results in total self-empowerment. In our increasingly mechanistic world, a more spiritual and *personal* approach is needed by us all. Candle-Lighting helps you fashion a personal approach with beauty, warmth and radiance.

Thinking Makes It So

Ancient and modern wisdom teaches that what you think about happens: *energy always follows thought*. This is a law of life, sometimes called the law of karma; and, as with the computer, once you master the way it works, you can achieve whatever you can conceive.

Our thoughts and words are actually "radioactive" energy that absolutely creates our world. You may think: "This [*you name it*] is not what I wanted at all." The reality of the situation is that you consciously or subconsciously thought or spoke your present experience. You need not *believe* this, since Universal Laws operate with or without our belief. We create the thoughts. We create the words. Therefore, we should create them positively, for the good of all.

The Lore of Candle-Lighting

Candle-Lighting is still used today for religious, personal and cultural purposes, just as it has been used since ancient times by the spiritually aware—advanced players in the Game of Life who know how to play it, and who play it well.

In ancient times, for example, Emperors and Kings strategically placed lit wax figurines of warriors on a fabricated background resembling our modern-day checkerboard. Calmly focused, they visualized and made the winning moves, ensuring victory in their campaigns.

The wise now, as then, use this most simple of tools, the Candle, to visualize and manifest — via affirmation, meditation or prayer — new conditions into their lives or to snuff out the old and unwanted thinking-patterns and their undesirable consequences.

Erase! Delete!
The truth being that "As you think, so shall you be," Candle-Lighting can be a powerful vehicle to help you create new positive thought-patterns or mental tapes while *simultaneously* erasing the old negative thought- pat-

9

terns, conscious or subconscious, that produce the very conditions that cause us unhappiness on every level—mental, spiritual and physical.

So much of what we repeatedly think and say has come not from *us* but from our environment—our families, the church, the schools, government, etc. All destructive information that we have accumulated since birth needs to be deleted and replaced by positive thought-patterns.

10

Once new thought-seeds are planted and germinate, we find that our lives change or "outpicture" simultaneously in amazingly positive ways. It just takes a mustard-seed of faith, concentration, willpower and patience. These states of mind are the landscaping plan for the garden of your life.

As you light the appropriately colored Candle for a certain goal or purpose, you begin the journey of lighting,

and therefore experiencing, your life as you desire it to
be. *You* create your life and everyone in it; *you* control it.
Candle-Lighting is a delightful vehicle with which to
bring positively controlled thought into concrete form.
Now you can truly know the joy of living.

First, Prepare Your Mind
The proper mental state must be established before you
begin the practice of Candle-Lighting. The first thing
to note is that *both* negative *and* positive thoughts work in
exactly the *same* way. This is because the Law of Cause
and Effect, the Law of Life, is always impersonal.

Think of the light-switch. *Anyone* can turn it On or Off
and get exactly the same result. The Law of Life is
impersonal and, like the light-switch, always says "Yes,"
whether you turn it On or Off—whether you plant a
positive or negative thought-seed. Your words and

thoughts will return to you fulfilled, since life creates according to your dictate.

Any thought, whether positive or negative, given enough energy, will manifest sooner or later. Realize that you are in total control of your life; you are in the driver's seat. To be a negative thinker is the equivalent of being a reckless driver. Therefore, you will daily practice the monitoring of your thoughts. This can seem strenuous at first, but, like good driving, it becomes increasingly automatic with practice.

Lighting with Words

With the lighting of each Candle it is always good to add a positive Affirmation or "Meditation" which can be silent or spoken. Why add it? Because positive repetition by the conscious mind becomes accepted by the subconscious mind, which then molds and shapes the

12

conscious command—positive or negative—as you think or speak it.

When this new thought or pattern is *permanently* planted in, and accepted by, the subconscious, it effortlessly reproduces this in outward form or circumstance. And again: as the new thought or pattern becomes permanent, the old negative thought-habit is simultaneously and permanently erased.

Note that fear and doubt are robbers of life, of positive energy, and are never to be entertained. In order to create and to heal, you must first relax and release all fear. An affirmation I use daily is:

I affirm that I am always one with Spirit [God] and therefore I am always successful, in perfect health and free from all fear.

The result is that you are now creating your new self—your life from a new clear and clean energy field. You will begin to notice that your experiences are becoming wonderfully positive. Negative associations and experiences are beginning to fade away.

You find that you prosper whatever you turn to, which makes you much more confident and happy in every way. You now experience the joy of self-empowerment. Whatever good you envision, you name it and claim it. You can create anything, for yourself and others—*and you now know it!*

Resistance and Release

Your mind (conscious and subconscious) may initially resist your new determination. Don't give this resistance energy! Resistance is part of the process. Persevere and you will definitely see your new ideas blossom into what you can touch and feel.

Closing the door on the past—forgiving and therefore being forgiven—embrace your glorious present and future. Nothing is too good to be true, *so do not compromise.* "Place your order" via Candle and Affirmation/ Meditation and wait patiently for it to be delivered. In the meantime, just do whatever brings you joy.

Happiness is also knowing when to let go, so: after you have placed your order—be confident—*and let it go!*

Remember, too: *You can always change your mind*; you don't have to stick with it. There are unlimited words and thoughts to choose from. Billions! And they *all* have unlimited power. Candle-Lighting is the art of *projected* positive thinking. With a little practice you can and will create a new and happy world for yourself.

Lighting Your Candle

CANDLES HAVE STRONG EMOTIONAL APPEAL. The light is soothing, making for a serene, comfortable atmosphere conducive to manifesting your good. And all of us benefit from the aid of color, which, like music, is a universal language—creative and healing.

Getting into the Spirit

You may like the idea of erecting a small altar in a room that is convenient and undisturbed. The altar need not be high off the ground. The lower it is, though, the more careful you will have to be. Remember, too, a burning candle should never be unattended, especially in the presence of children or pets. You may also want to burn incense, sing, dance or chant to create an atmosphere that uplifts, energizes and amplifies your energy field as you focus on the Candle flame, projecting your thought in its direction.

Candle-Lighting is the performance of inner (spiritual) work; therefore, you must be patient, centered, calm and focused. It is always helpful to practice deep breathing before you begin your session. I also recommend that you keep this work to yourself unless you are communicating with someone with whom you have this spiritual knowledge in common. Otherwise, it is best to keep it in the Silence.

You may wish to begin with something small and then graduate to larger goals. Or you can start at the top by shooting for the highest. *It's all up to you.* Play with it; have fun. Just remember to take the high road and stay on it, always working for the good of all. A negative thought energized will return to you—*with interest!* So stay positive.

Getting Started

The first thing to know is the appropriate Candle Color for the goal you wish to achieve. This is discussed in detail below. All colors vibrate at different frequencies and therefore function to create different effects. Always be sure to use the appropriate Candle Color to achieve your goal.

Combinations of Candle Colors are also very effective. Have fun and experiment. Use your intuition. For example, if you wish to move, lighting a combination of RED and GREEN Candles has proven to be an impetus to relocation. (See pp.25–49 for a discussion of the significance of the colors.)

First Steps

Be sure to use a *new* Candle and to avoid the touching or handling of your Candle by others. This helps keep the Candle in a virgin state until you "charge" or energize it with your vibration. (See this as mental, not physical.) To impregnate the new Candle with your personal energy, apply a light oil (with fragrance, if you wish) to your hand and gently massage the Candle.

Next, grasp the Candle with the left hand just below the midpoint—and just above the midpoint with the right hand. Hold this for a moment. Then, with a pair of scissors, lightly snip the top of the wick and light the Candle. Having thus been made "yours," the Candle is now at your service.

Lighting Your Color

YOUR INNATE SENSITIVITY to Color and its vibrations has already prepared you for the distinctions that Color can make in Candle-Lighting. Your subconscious then takes over, associating certain Colors with the different values, qualities and attitudes that you have in mind when you use Candle power. This means that you will want to use specific Colors for specific purposes. You will note, too, that sometimes the same work is done by more than one Color. And sometimes a *combination* of colors achieves a dramatic effect.

Keep in mind that the following guidelines for selecting color are meant to be *suggestive.* You will enjoy improvising and experimenting as you go along. Remember, too, that Candle-Lighting is an *inner* activity, and that your imaginative—sometimes even *playful*—spirit is definitely to be indulged!

23

GREEN represents Money. If Employment is your desire, light a GREEN Candle and command its manifestation. As with the other colors, you can think or speak aloud your Meditation via the Candle flame or write your wish on a piece of paper placed beneath the Candle. Prefer parchment to ordinary paper. The more *extra*ordinarily you work with Mind, the more *extra*ordinarily it will work with you. GREEN is also relevant to Plants and Gardens; Calming; Healing; Revitalizing.

GREEN MEDITATION 1: *I am Money. Infinite richness moves through me as boundless supply. Wonderfully liberating, empowering money descends like a downpour into my life, and all my affairs are benefited and prospered NOW. All thoughts of lack and limitation are loosed and let go, and I am rich and FREE. So it is!*

GREEN MEDITATION 2: *I am employed, and am **always** employed, by that Self of me that is greater than I am. I do not come into or fall out of its service; I am **always** there. It expresses as me and serves up continuously perfect opportunities, stimulating responsibilities, delightful conditions and generous compensation. I am happy, taking charge, taken care of and fulfilled. So it is!*

- Money
- Employment
- Plants & Gardens
- Calming
- Healing
- Revitalizing

PINK represents Love—emotional

rather than physical. Light a PINK Candle also to induce Peace of Mind; and it helps secure a Good Sleep. The deeper the PINK, the deeper the Love. PINK will also help attract Money and Prosperity in every form—because Love always attracts abundant *good energy,* in *every* form.

PINK MEDITATION 1: *I am Love. I am loving, and I am loved. Love works through me as my source and my outcome. I am Love in action. All non-loving thoughts and feelings find no place in me. Love goes forth from me and comes back to me multiplied. So it is!*

PINK MEDITATION 2: *I rest in perfect Sleep. Every thought and feeling is tranquil, every muscle and nerve is at total ease. "There is rest for the weary." No experience or memory robs me of what is mine. I leave this day behind in anticipation of a better tomorrow. Sleep ushers me into sweet repose, and I awake new and refreshed. So it is!*

- Love
- Peace of Mind
- Sleep
- Money
- Prosperity
- Good Energy

27

WHITE represents Protection;

Purity; Peace of Mind. Light a WHITE Candle also in any communication with the "Other Side."

WHITE MEDITATION 1: *I am Protection. I know that I am in the embrace of a Power greater than I am that keeps me from all danger and harm. "For underneath are the everlasting arms." I am not vulnerable or at risk of any kind. A circle of protection surrounds me and mine and all. So it is!*

WHITE MEDITATION 2: *I am Purity. There is not, nor can there be, anything that "stains" me. Nothing but good attaches itself to me, nothing but inner and outer beauty "marks" me. I proceed in life unblemished, untarnished, untainted. I am radiant Purity demonstrating itself as me. So it is!*

⟨29⟩

- ⟋ Protection
- ⟋ Purity
- ⟋ Peace of Mind
- ⟋ The "Other Side"

SILVER

represents the Clearing of
Energy Fields; Psychic
Protection; Repulsion of
Negative Energy; True
"Seeing." Light a SILVER
Candle for Detachment— the
ability to "let go."

SILVER MEDITATION 1: *I am Clear, and I know that I am clear. My mental and emotional vision is unobstructed and far-seeing. All dimness and obscurity are banished from my sight. All negative energy is spent. The Way lies straight before me, and I go in it. So it is!*

SILVER MEDITATION 2: *I am proof against all negative energy of whatever kind: it cannot touch, drain or influence me. I am surrounded by a sheath of Love that deflects the energies of all false thought and intention. "It shall not come nigh thee." I pass safely and freely on my way. So it is!*

31

Clearing Energy Fields
Psychic Protection
Repelling Negative Energy
True "Seeing"
Detachment
To "Let Go"

PURPLE represents Faith; Psychic Perception; Spiritual Insight. And light a PURPLE Candle for dealing with Legal Affairs or Protection.

PURPLE MEDITATION 1: *I am Faith. Deep, abiding certainty of my good is mine. All doubts and fears are dispelled; they have no substance and are powerless. I am solid as a fortress built upon a rock. My truth cannot be budged. My Faith is secure. My life is assured. So it is!*

PURPLE MEDITATION 2: *I am Insight into my own rich spiritual Being and that of all existence. I see through to the true cause and nature of all that exists and happens around me. No cloak of disunity, inharmony or sense of evil hides radiant Reality from me. I "judge righteous judgment": I affirm that only the Good is ultimately true. So it is!*

- Faith
- Psychic Perception
- Spiritual Insight
- Legal Affairs Protection

BLACK

Clearing of Blockages and Sidelining of Negative People. Light a BLACK Candle, therefore, if you need to to put a "stop" to, or separate from, undesirable people and conditions in your life. BLACK is a very powerful color and should be used with great caution, as the vibration can set up "backfire" unless used with unconditional Love and a sense of spiritual responsibility. PURPLE will usually do what is needed. If not, Use BLACK as a last resort.

BLACK MEDITATION 1: *I am Freedom from all blockage and impediments. Nothing in my life can weigh on me or restrict me. All negatives are gone, and I release all negative people to their own good. Only the good and the true has access to me, and I rejoice in my perfect freedom. So it is!*

BLACK MEDITATION 2: *I am Freedom from all those whose vibration contradicts the good, the harmonious, the whole. I am not heir to, subject to, or a party to their thought and feeling wavelengths. My thought brings to me those who live and move in positive ways, and my life is filled with them. The door is barred to all others. So it is!*

- ◆ Clearing Blockages
- ◆ Sidelining Negative People
- ◆ "Stop!" to Undesirable Conditions

ORANGE represents

Prosperity; Funds; Good Friends; Good Health (especially favorable Respiratory Conditions); Self-Esteem; Confidence; Material Abundance. You might say that ORANGE is the color for "breathing easy" in every way. And light an ORANGE Candle when you practice Yoga. (Also see BROWN, for ORANGE-BROWN.)

ORANGE MEDITATION 1: *I am Ease in my life and in my world. In every way I take things lightly, so my way is made easy and light. Nothing has power over me unless I grant it; therefore I withdraw all authority from burdens and claim sovereignty over my circumstances, declaring them a comfort and a joy. So it is!*

ORANGE MEDITATION 2: *I am perfect Health—of mind, of spirit and of body. I know that my physical me is whole and intact. Every cell, tissue, nerve, muscle, organ and bone of my body is bathed in the light of right order and harmony. I am unbowed by suggestions of contagion, illness or dysfunction. Instead I am alive with exuberant health and boundless energy. I rejoice that it is so!*

37

◆ Prosperity
◆ Funds
◆ Friends
◆ Health
◆ Self-Esteem
◆ Confidence
◆ Abundance
◆ Yoga

YELLOW represents

Communication—Writing and Creative Expression of all kinds, such as Music, Dance, Singing, Art, Acting—even Laughter. Light a YELLOW Candle where Children (*communication!*) are concerned. (Note this positive affirmation concerning Children: *My children are always happy, healthy and safe.*) And light a YELLOW Candle in dealing with arthritis.

YELLOW MEDITATION 1: *I am Expression being seen, heard and acknowledged. The lines of communication going out from me are strong and clear. There is no confusion, no misunderstanding, no ill will. I benefit and am benefited. I gladden and am made glad. It is good with me and my world. So it is!*

YELLOW MEDITATION 2: *I am the joyous Laughter of youth. I find great fun in life and leave tragedy to the tragic. Nothing is too good to be true; I don't take life over-seriously, and I find those who laugh at me the funniest people of all. So it is!*

- Communication
- Creative Expression
- Music
- Dance
- Singing
- Art
- Writing
- Acting
- Children
- Treating Arthritis

GOLD like PINK, represents Love: the Master Healer; Wealth; Powerful Friends; Associates; Inspiration; Confidence.

GOLD MEDITATION 1: *I am my own Inspiration. I am new Ideas. All right thoughts well up from within me and spill over into my affairs, healing them, remaking them and bringing them to fruition. Every void is filled; every perfect solution is provided; and every bright idea is already at work towards the perfect goal. So it is!*

GOLD MEDITATION 2: *I am a Friend. I draw to myself plenty of friends who see in me the Self that makes us one. My friends bless and benefit me, and knowing me blesses and benefits them. My associates are influences for good, and they advance all my rightful interests. I love them with the same Love with which they love me. It is so!*

- Love
- Healing
- Wealth
- Powerful Friends
- Associates
- Inspiration
- Confidence

BLUE

represents Peace; Harmony; Health; Friendship; Balance; Relaxation; Beautiful Surroundings; Bodies of Water. Light a BLUE Candle if your thought alights on Suburban/Country Living.

Blue Meditation 1: *I am Peace. All harmonious well-being is mine by divine right. "For this came I into the world." No conflict, ugliness or disorder finds a place in my experience. My surroundings reflect my inner balance, and everything around me takes its place as beauty and harmony. So it is!*

Blue Meditation 2: *I am Beauty, therefore I am surrounded by Beauty. Everything around me conspires to enhance, embellish and augment the splendor of a colorful cosmos. Because I see only the beautiful, the world reflects only Beauty back to me. So it is!*

43

- Peace
- Harmony
- Health
- Friendship
- Balance
- Relaxation
- Beautiful Surroundings
- Bodies of Water
- Country Living
- Suburban Living

BROWN represents Grounding;

Conservation of Earth and Animals; Working with the Hands. Light an ORANGE and a BROWN Candle together in your effort to become a non-smoker.

BROWN MEDITATION 1: *I am fully Grounded, on my own footing and in true form. Nothing has power to dislodge me from my right basis as I move through life responding to every duty and need. I am not swayed by others but am open and reasonable. I move in freedom and harmony, while always occupying high ground. So it is!*

BROWN MEDITATION 2: *I am a Friend to all life. The Intelligence and Feelings that find expression in animals are embraced by my own possession of these qualities, for they derive from one and the same Source. I cause no pain or suffering to animals but have at heart their welfare under the common roof of our planetary home. So it is!*

- Grounding
- Conservation
- Working with the Hands
- Stop Smoking

RED

represents the Magnetic, the Exciting, the Energizing; it stands for Gaining Rank; a Depression- Buster; the "Fighting Spirit"; Power—especially power for a woman if in the form of a red "image" Candle (candle in the shape of a woman).

RED MEDITATION 1: *I am Dynamic. I liven, and am enlivened by, everything around me. My energy is unlimited and irresistible. I am a force for good in every thought I think, every word I speak and everything I do. There is no drag on me, and I am never a drag on self or others. I am power to* do, *and to do* well. *So it is!*

RED MEDITATION 2: *I am depression-proof. I deny that my mind is the product of nerves or chemicals. I face and accept the fact that depression is a thing of thought; therefore I use my power of thought to say to depression: "Be gone! You are nothing but a fraudulent habit—a* nothing *acting like a* something. *I am the boss of my mind, the captain of my soul. This hijack is over as I now assert my authority. Be gone!" Mental composure and stability are mine. I claim their sovereignty in my life— and it is so!*

(47)

◆ Excitement
◆ Energizing
◆ Rank
◆ Depression
◆ Power
◆ "Fighting Spirit"
◆ Woman's Power

A NOTE ON SHOPPING FOR CANDLES

CANDLE-LIGHTING is immensely practical; but there is also an aesthetic aspect to it that you will want to cultivate for yourself. Candles can be very beautiful—and expensive—but this is a private matter. The size and shape and cost of a given Candle —and whether or not it is scented—are not essential to Candle-Lighting.

Candles are more popular today than at any time since the advent of gaslight and electricity. Their availability—in a variety of outlets, including Candle shops—is very widespread and convenient. Many mass-marketing stores (e.g. Target, Walmart) and super-markets have a Candle section, which often you can find by following your nose. Both the Internet and the Yellow Pages will point you in helpful directions. Also, Candle-making kits are available at your local crafts shop.

The Lottery is uncertain, but the results of the practice of Candle-Lighting are guaranteed, because you are not working superstitiously, but with *Cause and Effect*—call it karma—which is always *the* fact of life; and let us confine ourselves to another fact: that basing your practice of Candle-Lighting on pure unconditional Love energy will make you one of the happiest people on earth.

Index of Attributes

and their Respective Colors

Abundance ● Orange

Acting ● Yellow

Art ● Yellow

Arthritis, Treating ● Yellow

Associates ● Gold

Balance ● Blue

Beautiful Surroundings ● Blue

Blockages, Clearing ● Black

Bodies of water ● Blue

Calming ● Green

Children ● Yellow

Clearing Energy Fields ● Silver

Clearing of Blockages ● Black

Communication ● Yellow

Communication with
   the "Other Side" ● White

Confidence ●● Orange, Gold

Conservation ● Brown

Country Living ● Blue

Creative Expression ● Yellow

Dance ● Yellow

Depression ● Red

Detachment ● Silver

Earth ● Brown

Employment ● Green

Energizing ● Red

Energy Fields ● Silver

Energy, Good ● Pink

Energy, Negative ● Silver

Excitement ● Red

Expression, Creative ● Yellow

Faith ● Purple

"Fighting Spirit" ● Red

Friends ● Orange, Gold

Friendship ● Blue

Funds ● Orange

Gardens ● Green

Good Energy ● Pink

Good Friends ● Orange

Good Health ● Orange

Grounding ● Brown
Hands, Working with ● Brown
Harmony ● Blue
Healing ● ● Green, Gold
Health ● Orange
Inspiration ● Gold
Legal Affairs ● Purple
Let Go, to ● Silver
Love ● ● Pink, Gold
"Magnetic," the ● Red
Money ● Green, Pink
Music ● Yellow
Negative Energy ● Silver
Negative People ● Black
Non-smoker, to be a ● Brown
"Other Side," the ● White
Peace ● Blue
Peace of Mind ● ● Pink, White
Plants ● Green
Power ● Red
Power, a Woman's ● Red
Powerful Friends ● Gold
Prosperity ● ● Pink, Orange
Protection ● ● White, Purple
Protection, Psychic ● Silver

Psychic Perception ● Purple
Psychic Protection ● Silver
Purity ● White
Rank ● Red
Relaxation ● Blue
Repelling Negative Energy ● Silver
Respiratory Conditions ● Orange
Revitalizing ● Green
"Seeing," True ● Silver
Self-Esteem ● Orange
Sidelining Negative People ● Black
Singing ● Yellow
Sleep ● Pink
Stop Smoking ● Brown
Spiritual Insight ● Purple
"Stop!" to Undesirable
    Conditions ● Black
Suburban Living ● Blue
True "Seeing" ● Silver
Undesirable Conditions ● Black
Wealth ● Gold
Woman's Power ● Red
Working with the Hands ● Brown
Writing ● Yellow
Yoga ● Orange